Cultural Dilemmas

Controversial Issues To Stretch Your Mind

異文化の戸惑い

by

Masamichi Asama

and

Colin Sloss

EIHŌSHA

テキストの音声は、弊社 HP
http://www.eihosha.co.jp/の
「テキスト音声ダウンロード」
のバナーからダウンロードでき
ます。

は　し　が　き

　2003 年 1 月に初めて本書（原作）を著してから早 15 年の歳月が経とうとしています．原作テキスト執筆の契機は，2001 年 9 月 11 日に米国で引き起り，世界を震撼させたあの同時多発テロに由来しましたが，その後ますます世界を取り巻く情勢は混迷を深めつつあるように思えてなりません．不安定な中東および朝鮮半島情勢に端を発する国際紛争の危険性，地球温暖化に起因する異常気象の猛威と局地的被害，英国の EU 離脱による国際バランスの懸念，新たなタイプの国家リーダー出現によるポピュリズムの台頭，クローン技術ほかの進展による「神」の領域に足を踏み入れつつある医療技術，世界的規模での貧富の差の拡大など，まさに人類は今大いなる試練に直面していると言っても過言ではありません．本書の日本語題『異文化の戸惑い』がますます現実味を帯びてきているようです．

　そのような状況を踏まえ，今般初版の内容を大きく差し替えて *Cultural Dilemmas* の名の下に装いを新たにして本書を著すことにいたしました．あらためて現在国際社会の中で顕在化しつつある様々な問題の深層に視線を注いで欲しいと願う次第です．と同時に，自らの目線で問題解決の拠り所をも探索してもらえればと念ずる次第です．

　さて，本テキストにおいては今回，練習問題もより時宜に合う形に改編いたしました．A. B. のリスニング問題はそれぞれの Chapter のテーマに沿いながらも TOEIC を意識した問題に改編しました．2016 年 6 月に導入された新形式版のスタイルも一部反映してあります．奥深い内容理解と合わせて，より実用的なリスニング練習にも親しんでもらえるよう工夫いたしました．また，和文英訳問題も，全面改訂し，難解な和文英訳作業に対峙しながらもいくつかの Cue をヒントに発想を絞り込んでゆくスタイルを採用しました．本文中の言い回しをヒントに，応用英作文のスキルを磨いていただけたら幸いです．

　最後に，本テキストの作成に際しましては英宝社の佐々木元社長，そして橋本稔寛氏，下村幸一氏には並々ならぬご尽力をいただきました．ここに厚く感謝申し上げる次第です．

2018 年 2 月吉日

淺　間　正　通

CONTENTS

Chapter 1　The Paradox of International Tourism 7
（海外旅行のパラドックス）

Chapter 2　The Sensitive Kind 13
（過敏な類の人々）

Chapter 3　The Age of Robots 19
（ロボット全盛の時代）

Chapter 4　The Big Problem 25
（問題の中に潜む問題）

Chapter 5　To Buy or Not To Buy 31
（買うべきか，買わざるべきか）

Chapter 6　Suicidal Tendencies 37
（自爆テロの内側）

Chapter 7　Behind the Veil 43
（ヴェールに覆われた価値観）

Chapter 8　Women Are Not from Venus, Men Are Not from Mars . . 49
（すれ違う幻想，「男らしさ」と「女らしさ」）

Chapter 9　Crime and Punishment 55
（罪と罰，その本質論）

Chapter 10　All Jamaicans Love Reggae Music 61
（異文化ステレオタイプ）

Chapter 11　The Internet 67
（インターネットの功罪）

Chapter 12　Living on Fiji Time 73
（フィジーの時の流れに学ぶ）

Chapter 13　Affirmative Action 79
（積極的差別解消策は善か悪か）

Chapter 14　The Diversity of Lying 85
（許される嘘，許されざる嘘）

Chapter 15　Talking With a Child About Cancer 91
（小児がん告知の背景）

Chapter 1

The Paradox of International Tourism

A British person, living in America, was once visited by some friends from Britain. He took them to various places to see the sights. Wherever they went, his friends kept asking him anxiously, "Is this the real America?" The puzzled man could only reply "Yes, this is America."

This story nicely illustrates what we could call "the paradox of tourism." When we visit foreign countries as tourists, we tend to be determined to see the real or authentic aspects of that country; the "Japaneseness" of Japan or the "Indianness" of India. However, with increasing globalization, what represents the "real" aspects of a particular culture has become harder to identify. For example, a *karaoke* bar in the Philippines has become just as much a part of that country as, say, a McDonald's has become a part of the culture of Japan.

Nevertheless, tourists often go to great lengths to seek out the "real" in the countries they visit. However, sometimes the "real" proves to be unsatisfactory and tourists have to recreate the country to match their own expectations. For example, when visiting Thailand tourists might feel rather uncomfortable in the polluted urban sprawl that is present-day Bangkok. Instead, they could feel much happier when they visit the beautiful island-resorts to the south. They might feel that

20 they had discovered the real Thailand. Soon though, they might start to notice that the island is full of foreigners and that the only Thai people to be seen are either serving food or selling something. This is because the resort is actually "Thailand" as foreigners would like to have it.

Some complain that tourists by their very presence change or even
25 ruin the countries they visit. This helps to explain the endless quest of tourists to find more remote and unspoilt places; an ultimately hopeless endeavour in a finite world. This is a self-defeating, but understandable, desire to escape from one's own culture.

We can recently find in Japan a possible alternative to the problem
30 of tourism. This involves the creation of theme parks with names like "Spain Village." At such places people can enjoy the simulation of a foreign country while avoiding some of the unpleasant realities of foreign travel. Unfortunately though, we also lose what seems to be the greatest benefit of foreign travel: the way it forces us to question
35 our assumptions and stereotypes.

NOTES

2 **See the sights**「名所を見物する；観光する」(cf. sightseeing 名詞)

4 **puzzled** = confused

5 **illustrates**「〜を例証している」

6– **be determined to ~**「断固として〜しようとする」(ex. She is determined to succeed.)

7 **the real or authentic aspects of that country**「その国の本当の様子（様相）」(real/authentic = genuine)

10 **identify**「〜（が何であるか）を明らかにする」

11– **just as much part of that country as ~**「〜とちょうど同じくらいその国の一部である」

12 **say** = for example

13 **go to great lengths to seek out**「徹底的に〜を探し出そうとする」

15 **recreate the country to match their own expectations**「自分たちの期待に合わせようとしてその国のイメージを再形成する」

17 **polluted urban sprawl** [sprɔ́ːl]「汚染された都市の雑然とした広がり」

20 **though**（adverb）＝ nevertheless　このthoughは接続詞ではなく，副詞であることに注意．

23 **"Thailand" as foreigners would like to have it**「外国人がそうであってほしいと願うような『タイ』」引用符の使用によって，いわゆる"タイ"，すなわち素顔のイメージの中で描くタイという気持ちが伝わる．

24 **by their very presence**「まさしく彼らがいることによって」（ex. The very thought of that incident makes me upset.）

25 **ruin**「台無しにする」（＝ spoil，したがって unspoilt は「あるがままの；自然のままの」という意味になる．）

25– **the endless quest of tourists to ~**「しようとする観光客の果てしない追求」

26– **an ultimately hopeless endeavour in a finite world**「限りある世界での，究極的に見込みのない努力」（米語では endeavor と綴られる．）

29– **a possible alternative to the problem of tourism**「観光旅行の問題に代わり得る手段」

34– **the way it forces us to question our assumptions and stereotypes**「それ（＝海外旅行）によって私たちが，いや応なしに，自分たちの思い込みや固定観念に疑いを抱くようになる有様」

EXERCISES

A. Listen and choose the sentence that best describes each picture.

1.　（A）　（B）　（C）　（D）　　2.　（A）　（B）　（C）　（D）

10 Cultural Dilemmas

B. Listen and choose the best response to each question or statement.

1. (A) (B) (C)   2. (A) (B) (C)   3. (A) (B) (C)

C. Draw lines joining words similar in meaning.

anxious   ·   ·   spoilt
determined   ·   ·   recognize
authentic   ·   ·   worried
identify   ·   ·   resolute
ruined   ·   ·   true

D. In which order do these sentences form the correct paragraph?

(A) Then, our stereotype about the Chinese and bicycles might be confirmed if we visited the capital city of Beijing which is a city of bicycles.

(B) The paradox of international tourism is above all a question of our perceptions of foreign cultures and the gap between those perceptions and reality.

(C) On visiting a large Chinese city like Dalian, however, we might be surprised to see numerous cars and very few bicycles because Dalian has many steep slopes.

Chapter 1 The Paradox of International Tourism 11

（D） For example, we might have the idea that most Chinese people ride to work or school on bicycles and that few people can afford their own car.

☐ → ☐ → ☐ → ☐

E. Translate the following Japanese sentences into English.

(1) 外国を訪れる観光旅行者たちは，しばしばその国の現実の姿に接して戸惑うことがあります.

_____when

they see authentic aspects of the country.

(2) ある人たちは実際の海外旅行の代替として，異国情緒豊かなテーマパークを訪れたりします.

Some people visit _____

_____ .

Chapter 2

The Sensitive Kind

The expression "politically correct" is sometimes used in the media to mean "silly overreaction." For example, it could be argued that the African people who object to the way African children are represented in the old children's story "Little Black Sambo" are taking the book for children too seriously. Or, the female newscaster, who complained that she was fired because of a perception that she had become too fat, might be accused of being "too" politically correct.

One strange thing about the term "politically correct" is that although it is sometimes used to label certain people, no one ever seems to admit that they themselves believe in the philosophy of political correctness. The term is frequently used in a negative sense and is often used as a means of avoiding serious debate about a particular issue.

Another problem is that a blanket condemnation of all attempts to be more sensitive to the feelings of others by calling all such attempts "political correctness" risks grouping genuine problems with seemingly

ridiculous complaints. "Politically correct" has developed such a negative connotation in the minds of most people that it might be best to abandon the expression entirely. This would leave us free to judge the complaints of minorities on their merits and demerits. One useful
20 rule to have might be: "If the person we are talking about objects to the words we use to describe them, then we had better not use those words."

However, there is a problem with trying to satisfy everyone. It is possible that by trying not to offend everyone, our conversation
25 may become over-serious and humourless. Here the Japanese may have something to teach the world. In formal business situations and meetings the Japanese often strike other nationalities as being too serious. There is some truth to this but it does sometimes help them to avoid misunderstanding and offending others. This is particularly true in
30 cross-cultural situations when it is easy to offend unintentionally. However, as no one can be serious all the time, the Japanese really let off steam with friends at parties. At such times the taboos and restraints of formal situations seem to completely disappear. The Japanese may have solved the problem of political correctness by placing great
35 importance on context.

NOTES

見出し **Sensitive**「過敏な；神経質な」

1 **"politically correct"**「（人種別，性別などの差別廃止の立場で）政治的に妥当である；公正さを期したPC，P.C と略して使うこともある.」

2 **"Silly overreaction"**「ばかげた過剰反応」

4 **"Little Black Sambo"** 南アフリカのHelen Bannerman（1927）が書いた絵本.

7– **might be accused of being "too" politically correct**「あまりにも PC にこだわ

りすぎていると非難されるかもしれない」

10 **philosophy**「見解；考え方」

11 **exclusively** = only

13 **a blanket condemnation of ~**「～を（一切合財）なんでもかんでも非難することは」（cf. a blanket ban 全面禁止）

15– **risks grouping genuine problems with seemingly ridiculous complaints**「本当の問題をばかげた不平であると思われるものと一緒にしてしま

Chapter 2 The Sensitive Kind

	う危険を冒す」	24	**offend**「〜を怒らせる」
17	**connotation**「言外」に持つ意味	27	**strike ~ as ...** to give 〜 a particular impression（ex. She struck me as a very thoughtful person.）
18	**abandon the expression entirely** その表現（を使うこと）を全くやめる（ex. They have abandoned the scheme altogether.） **leave ~ free to ...**「〜を…するのを自由にさせておく」	31–	**let off steam**「（口語）うっぷんを晴らす」
18	**judge the complaints of minorities on their merits and demerits**「小数集団の不満を，それらの真価で判断する」ここでの merits は，"真価"，"実態" という意味．	33–	**the taboos and restraints of formal situations**「正式な場面の（もつ）タブーや制約」
		34–	**by placing great importance on context**「状況に大変重きをおくことによって」

EXERCISES

A. Listen and choose the sentence that best describes each picture.

1.　(A)　(B)　(C)　(D)　　2.　(A)　(B)　(C)　(D)

16 Cultural Dilemmas

B. Listen to the conversation and choose the best response to each question.

1. What does the woman have in her hand?

   (A) A map
   (B) A CD
   (C) A dictionary
   (D) A book

2. What does it joke about?

   (A) About someone's personality
   (B) About someone's habit
   (C) About someone's appearance
   (D) About someone's behavioral pattern

3. What does the man want to do now?

   (A) To tell a joke about her
   (B) To hear one more joke from her
   (C) To make a joke of himself
   (D) To share the joke she told him

Chapter 2 The Sensitive Kind   17

C. Spell out the words defined below.

1. ( )i( )o( )ity:
    a smaller group which is different from the larger, controlling
    group in race, religion, etc.
2. ( )e( )( )iti( )e:
    knowing or being conscious of the feelings and opinions of others
3. ( )ve( )( )eac( ):
    to act in a highly emotional way beyond what seems called for
4. ( )on( )e( )t:
    the whole situation, background, or environment relevant to a
    particular event
5. ( )on( )o( )a( )ion:
    the ideas suggested by a word in addition to its explicit meaning

D. In which order do these sentences form the correct paragraph?

(A) The expression "politically correct" is often used to suggest that
     someone's thinking lacks sophistication and that they have been
     overly sensitive about a particular issue.

(B) Perhaps we can conclude that the expression "politically
     correct" is too vague in the way it generalizes about a number of
     important differences.

(C) Sometimes there is some truth in such a suggestion, particularly
     when people tend to exaggerate differences amongst people and
     cultures and ignore the similarities.

(D) Unfortunately, there are also cases when a genuine problem is ignored by the thinking and excessive use of this vague and unhelpful expression.

☐ → ☐ → ☐ → ☐

E. Translate the following Japanese sentences into English.

(1) もし我々がPC（政治的公正さ）の問題を真剣に受けとめすぎてしまうならば，日常会話にユーモアがなくなってしまいます．

_____ ,

our conversation would be humorless.

(2) 外国人は「ガイジン」と呼ばれると，しばしば不快感を露わにします．

_____ when someone

calls them "gaijin".

Chapter 3

The Age of Robots

In our daily lives we can already notice a lot of robots. Robots are involved in the manufacture of many products such as transportation vehicles. Since flying robots, called drones, are cheap and useful, many people have been buying them recently. Robots with an installed camera can photograph many things. They are essential during nuclear disasters like that in Fukushima, as they can take pictures of a melted-down reactor, something which people cannot do safely.

Robots can also be effective in war. For instance, in South Korea an arms maker has created a robotic gun turret which can see and shoot. In addition to such general defence purposes, it is likely that the military would like to use robots to fight extremists.

Japan is a land of robots. Many universities have competitions to see who can build the best ones. However, this isn't totally academic experimentation, because in a rapidly aging society, robots could be of great help. During a recent lecture, a post-graduate student claimed robots could have a breath sensor installed which could tell if an elderly person had eaten any vegetables that day or not. Also they could help with the heavy lifting which is necessary in caring for the elderly, reducing the number of nurses necessary for such tasks.

20   Japan has also developed socially interactive robotics. For example, "Pepper" has been invented in Japan. This is the world's first robot designed to live with humans. Pepper can communicate, and responds to human moods: when you are happy, Pepper is happy; when you are sad, Pepper is sad. You might think this is just a gimmick, but Pepper 25 has been very successful. Within the first minute following its sales launch, 1,000 Peppers made by Aldebaran Robots and Softbank sold out. And on a more frivolous note, Japan even has a robot hotel!

    One additional type of robot may make all our lives better in the future. Self-driving cars have become better and better, so perhaps in 30 the future, instead of driving ourselves, we can read a book or watch a movie while a robotic vehicle takes us to our destinations. If for no other reason, many people would appreciate a robotic car which could park for them like a parking valet at a hotel. There are, of course, safety factors to consider, but great progress has already been made. Possibly in 35 the future you won't need to pass a driving test (though driving schools would no doubt be unhappy about that development). Although this seems like science fiction, we are getting closer to such a time. One day it is likely your child will say, 'Mummy, Daddy, what is a car license?'

    Despite these promising uses, some people are questioning issues 40 related to safety and privacy when thinking about the growing impact of robots within human societies. In the former case, movies such as Terminator propose military or policing uses and, while such movies are popular, they project a future in which humans are controlled by robots. In another example, *2001: A Space Odyssey*, a computer goes crazy 45 and kills off people. So this is always a fundamental dilemma: we need robots, but we are a little nervous about them. While we can control them now, perhaps they will control us in the future. It is a bit like a

Chapter 3 The Age of Robots

fear of aliens: if such a creature exists, and it is much cleverer than us, why wouldn't it eat us?! In a similar vein, there is a fear that robots will be able to access personal information without human knowledge or approval —with the result that they could exploit such information at human expense.

One cause of such fear is that recently a robot has passed a self-awareness test. This test, called the 'wise-man puzzle' imagines a situation where three people have a hat placed on their heads from behind and the winner is the first to guess the colour. This scenario is adapted for three robots who are told that two of them have been given a 'dumbing pill'. One robot responds, changing his answer mid-sentence to reflect that only he had not received this pill. Until this point, no robot had demonstrated a sense of self-awareness. For people who mistrust robotics, the result of this experiment is unnerving and frightening.

NOTES

- **drone**「（無線操縦の）無人航空機」
- **reactor**「原子炉」(= nuclear reactor)
- **turret**「回転式砲塔」
- **extremist**「（特に政治上の）極端論者；過激主義者」
- **a breath sensor**「呼気センサー」
- **Pepper**「ペッパー」
  感情認識ヒューマノイドタブレット．ソフトバンクロボティクス株式会社が販売などの事業展開を手掛けており，ヒト型ロボットとして店舗などへの導入が進んでいる．
- **a gimmick**「（人目をひくための）工夫；新手」
- **Aldebaran Robot**「アルデバランロボティクス社のロボット」
  アルデバランロボティクス社はフランスのパリに本社を置き，自律型

ヒューマノイド・ロボット Nao の設計，生産，販売を中心とする事業を行うソフトバンクグループ傘下の企業．

- **frivolous**「取るに足らない」(n. frivolousness)
- **a parking valet**「（ホテル・レストランなどの）駐車係」．
- **dilemma** = a choice of two answers or actions, both of which seem difficult or bad; a difficult choice
- **in a similar vein**「同じように」
- **exploit**「開発する；（情報を）引き出す」
- **self-awareness**「自己認識」
- **a 'dumbing pill'**「言語能力を失わせる薬」
- **unnerving**「驚かされる」

EXERCISES

A. Listen and choose the sentence that best describes each picture.

1. (A)　(B)　(C)　(D)　　2. (A)　(B)　(C)　(D)

B. Listen to the conversation and choose the best response to each question.

1. What are they talking about?

   (A)　Online shopping
   (B)　Shopping malls
   (C)　Robotics
   (D)　A birthday present

2. What did the woman probably get from her husband last year?

   (A)　A dog
   (B)　A necklace
   (C)　A ticket to a beauty salon
   (D)　Flowers

3. What do the man and the girl think about the woman?

(A)　She is lazy.
(B)　She is tired.
(C)　She is talkative.
(D)　She is romantic.

C. Draw lines joining words opposite in meaning.

essential	·	·	serious
wise	·	·	fact
frivolous	·	·	young
elderly	·	·	unnecessary
fiction	·	·	silly

D. In which order do these sentences form the correct paragraph?

(A) If you were to keep a pet, which would you prefer: a living creature or a pet robot?

(B) Nowadays, some of these advanced robots are used as conversation partners for elderly people.

(C) Since then, pet robots have advanced greatly. A recent one is able to learn and develop by communicating with users.

(D) The first pet robot, "AIBO," attracted attention in 1999.

24   Cultural Dilemmas

E. Translate the following Japanese sentences into English.

(1) 雇用者は不平を言いがちな人間を雇う代わりに，人間が出来ない
ことをやれるロボットに依存することを選ぶかもしれません.

_____, instead of

hiring those who are likely to complain.

(2) もし人間生活に適応したヒト型人工知能ロボットが増えてくると
したら，共生できるように努力する必要があります.

If we should have more humanoid artificial intelligence robots

that are adapted for life together with humans, _____

_____.

Chapter 4

The Big Problem

When Feodor Dostoevski, the Russian writer, wrote about the great problem of the age in the nineteenth century, he was writing about the clash between religious and scientific thought at the time. Today, we too have many problems. The main issue we have with our problems is deciding which one is the most important.

From a global perspective there are certain problems that, most people probably would agree, transcend cultural differences. Global warming would seem to be a threat to everyone living on the planet, although, of course, some countries are under a more immediate threat than others. The dangers inherent in nuclear weapons and nuclear power plants would seem to be a worldwide problem. The problems caused by pollution also appear to transcend national boundaries. Advances in science also present us with moral and ethical problems related to such things as cloning, surrogate birth, and genetically modified foods.

Other problems are related to gaps in culture and wealth between nations. For example, in many countries overpopulation is seen as a major problem, while in other places like Western Europe and Japan it is the decline in population which is perceived as the main problem. So, we could argue that population imbalance is a global problem.

To deal with these problems some people advocate that we should increase cooperation. This would perhaps eventually lead to a World Government. Other more cynical people fear that global government would lead to global corruption on a massive scale.

All the problems discussed above are complex and it is clear that we are living in a complicated world. It is tempting when faced with such problems to rely on the opinions of experts who spend their lives dealing with a particular aspect of a certain problem. However, we may not want to rely on specialists who may be focusing on one tiny aspect of the problem, and, may not be able "to see the wood for the trees." On the other hand, we can not fully trust in politicians who claim to be able to see "the big picture." Unfortunately, neither of these options are really adequate. We remain with our problem about the problems.

NOTES

1 **Feodor Dostoevski**「ドストエフスキー」(1821–81) ロシアの小説家.

3 **clash** = a serious difference; a conflict

7 **transcend cultural differences**「文化の違いを超えて」

8 **live on the planet** = live on the earth

10 **inherit [ɪnhí(ə)rənt] in ~**「〜に内在する」

14 **surrogate birth**「代理出産」

15 **genetically modified foods**「遺伝子組みかえ食品」

19 **perceive ~ as ...**「〜を…と認識する」
(ex. I perceived her comment as a sign

of hostility.)

20 **imbalance**「不均衡」

21 **advocate** [ǽdvəkət]「主張する」

22 **eventually** = in the end

23 **cynical**「冷笑的な」(n. cynic)

24 **corruption**「汚職」(v. corrupt)
on a massive scale「大規模に」

26 **tempting** = attractive ; inviting
when faced with ~「〜と直面した時」
この face は他動詞であり，when のあとに we are を補うとわかりやすい.

30– **not be able "to see the wood for the**

Chapter 4 The Big Problem   27

> trees"「木を見て森を見ず；小事にとらわれて大局を見失う」
> 32　see "the big picture"「全体像を見る；対局をとらえる」
> 34　**adequate** = sufficient
> **We remain with our problem about the problems.**「私たちは，問題についての問題をかかえたままである.」

EXERCISES

A. Listen and choose the sentence that best describes each picture.

1.　（A）　（B）　（C）　（D）　　2.　（A）　（B）　（C）　（D）

B. Listen and choose the best response to each question or statement.

1.　（A）　（B）　（C）　　2.　（A）　（B）　（C）　　3.　（A）　（B）　（C）

C. Change the order of letters in the word according to each definition.

1. tvpreeepcis
    the way in which a situation or problem is judged

2. therenin:
    present naturally as a part of something

3. anpoew:
    a tool used to fight with, such as a sword, gun, or bomb

4. lionpupoat:
    the number of people living in a particular area, country

5. cooprutrin:
    dishonest or immoral behavior by the people in positions of power such as politicians

D. In which order do these sentences form the correct paragraph?

(A) This is why it has become of vital importance for us to identify the key problems, in particular, those problems which most urgently demand our attention.

(B) We are confronted with a growing number of different problems as technology develops and humans struggle to keep up with moral and ethical solutions to such problems in an increasingly complex world.

(C) Nevertheless, even with inadequate knowledge, it is sometimes necessary for us to try to use our imagination and instincts in an attempt to come up with solutions while there is still time.

(D) However, this is more easily said than done, because some of the moral and ethical implications of some scientific developments have yet to be fully understood.

E. Translate the following Japanese sentences into English.

(1) 人間のクローンを作ることは予測できない社会的，倫理的な問題を含んでいます．

_____ involves _____

_____ .

(2) 専門家によると，地球温暖化により海面上昇が引き起こり，将来水没してしまう国があるそうです．

Some experts say that _____

_____ and some countries might become flooded.

Chapter 5

To Buy or Not To Buy

A long while ago in Japan there was a flurry of books published concerning the same subject. The first was "You Shouldn't Buy This" (*kattewaikenai*). Later other books, some supporting and others criticising the original book, were published.

The theme of the book—the safety of the food we are eating— ought to be of interest to everybody. However, there are a number of important problems concerning this book. Firstly, was the author of the book saying that only the foods mentioned in the book were dangerous? Were all other foods not mentioned in the book, then, safe? The book was fairly well written with a lot of seemingly convincing scientific facts to back up the arguments. The trouble is another book was soon published in which another writer, who seemed to be an expert as well, also used scientific evidence to criticise the conclusions of the first book. This is a very interesting and significant problem. When we listen to the arguments of two experts who disagree about an important subject, how are we, if we lack a specialist knowledge of the subject, able to decide which expert is right?

Recently, people have become, justifiably, worried about such things as genetically modified foods, cloned meat and chemicals used to preserve food. People have noticed that fruit bought in supermarkets doesn't seem to go bad even when it gets old. Experts tell us that such food is perfectly safe, but have they really tested the effect of such food on the human body if one eats this kind of food every day for the next twenty years? Of course not, because such testing would cost too much and would take too much time.

Another point of view argues that we have a moral duty to eat such foods. This argument states that only by using such scientifically produced foods can we feed all the people in the world, some of whom are now starving. According to this position, if we insist on natural, organically grown food, we are condemning some people to death by starvation.

Some modern thinkers warn us to avoid making universal generalizations. However, in the face of this present-day information overload, perhaps we can be allowed to make the following one: today most people are struggling with the problem of too many questions and not enough answers.

Chapter 5 To Buy or Not To Buy

NOTES

見出し **To Buy or Not to Buy** "To be or not to be — that is the question." というShakespeareのハムレットの有名な一節にかけたもの.

1 **flurry** = a lot of things arriving or happening at once (ex. a flurry of letters) flurry は, もともと「突然おこる風, 雨, 雪」を意味する.

10 **fairly** = rather, quite

10– **seemingly convincing scientific facts**「印象深くて仰々しいほどの（鳴り者入りの）科学的真実」

18 **justifiably** = with good reason「もっともなことに；当然のことながら」

19– **cloned meat**「クローン牛」

chemicals used to preserve food = preservative「防腐剤」

21 **go bad** = rotten

22 **the effect of such food on the human body**「このような食品のもたらす人体への影響」

29 **starve** = to suffer or die from great hunger (n. starvation)

29 **organically grown**「有機肥料で栽培された」

condemn ~ to ... = to make ~ endure or accept a situation, etc. that they do

31 **making universal generalizations**「普遍的に一般化すること；あまねく一般化すること」

EXERCISES

A. Listen and choose the sentence that best describes each picture.

1. (A) (B) (C) (D)   2. (A) (B) (C) (D)

34   Cultural Dilemmas

B. Listen to the guestions and circle the correct answer.

CD
O
16

Q1: _____

(A) The topic of the book interests people but the content of the book suggests further problems.

(B) After the original book was published, only the books which criticized the original were published.

(C) People are not very interested in the arguments outlined in the books.

Q2: _____

_____

(A) Readers may have no specialist knowledge of the subject for making a judgement.

(B) The writers aren't specialists of the subject.

(C) Not all people tried to read both books. Therefore, they can only see one side of the problems.

Q3: _____

_____

(A) Because it may be too extravagant if you want to eat only naturally grown food.

Chapter 5 To Buy or Not To Buy   35

(B) Because we can find out the effect of such food on humans by continuing to eat it.

(C) Because only by eating such food is it possible to feed all the people in the world.

C. Spell out the words defined below.

1. ( )xp( )( )t:
    a person with special skill or knowledge which comes from experience or training

2. p( )e( )er( )e:
    to treat food in such a way that it can be kept a long time

3. ( )on( )e( )n:
    to force somebody into an unhappy state or situation

4. ( )( )rn:
    to tell of something bad that may happen, or of how to prevent something bad

5. s( )ru( )( )le:
    to make great efforts when trying to deal with a different problem or situation

D. In which order do these sentences form the correct paragraph?

(A) First, we should increase our basic knowledge of the subject we are interested in, because, as the saying goes, "a little information is better that none at all."

(B) There is no simple answer to this vital question as we live in an age of information overload with experts on various subjects continuously contradicting each other.

(C) As ordinary non-experts, what are we to do in the light of this barrage of conflicting and confusing information?

(D) Perhaps the greatest problem which faces consumers today is: How can we trust the producers of food and be sure that the food we eat is really good for us?

E. Translate the following Japanese sentences into English.

(1) 書店を訪れると、それぞれの科学的根拠を提示した異なる見解の健康指南書がたくさん並んでいるのに気づきます。

When we visit bookstores, we find a number of books on health with different perspectives, many of which _____.

(2) 遺伝子組み換え食品によって食糧不足で苦しむ人々を救える一方で、その食品の安全性を疑問視する人たちもいます。

_____,

some people are dubious about the safety of such food.

Chapter 6

Suicidal Tendencies

Recently in the media there has been much news about suicide bombers. Such suicide bombers strike fear in the minds of people in general precisely because they are prepared to sacrifice their own lives and the lives of others for their cause. People who are willing to sacrifice their own lives in such a way tend to inspire confused feelings of fear and a sometimes misplaced admiration for the suicide bomber's sincerity or purity of belief.

Being willing to die for your cause is not just a modern phenomenon. During the Seige of Malta 1565, one of the fiercest battles of all time, both the Christian Knights of St John and the Moslem Janissaries, the strongest soldiers in the Ottoman army, believed that they would go to heaven if they died in battle. Such strong faith in their religions created very strong fighters on both sides.

More recently the Japanese Kamikaze pilots in the Second World War caused great fear in the American forces towards the end of the war. There is a great poignancy in the idea of young men having to give up their lives at such an early age.

Suicide bombing sometimes occurs in conflicts among people who share the same religious belief, as was the case in the Iraq-Iran conflict. One of the controversial aspects of that conflict was that children were sometimes sacrificed in suicide attacks. It has been noticed that children are often more susceptible to the mental conditioning usually given to people before they are asked to sacrifice their lives for a particular cause.

Taking part in suicide missions against people of another religion or culture is without doubt the opposite of attempting to communicate and find understanding with people of other cultures. In the same way that war is said to represent the failure of diplomacy, such actions proclaim that force is the most important factor in the world and that the ends of one's actions justify the means. There is also a great deal of arrogance in the idea that one's cause is totally right and that one's enemy is totally wrong. Ultimately, to be willing to kill yourself and your enemy for a cause reveals a poverty of imagination.

NOTES

1– **suicide bombers** 「自爆テロ犯」(cf. suicide bombing)

2　**strike fear** 「恐怖に陥れる」

7　**purity** = the quality of being innocent and morally good（adj. pure）

9　**the Siege of Malta** 「マルタ包囲」(cf. the Siege of Corinth 「コリント包囲」 the Siege of the Rhodes 「ロードス島包囲」)

　　fierce = violent and angry

10　**Knights of St. John** 「聖ヨハネ騎士団」(= Nights Hospitalers)

Janissaries 「イェニチェリ（オスマン帝国下のトルコ軍の精鋭部隊の隊員）」

11　**Ottoman** 「オスマン帝国の」

12　**faith in** ~ = firm belief in ~

16　**poignancy** 「胸が痛む」(adj. poignant)

18　**conflicts** = war and battles

22　**susceptible** 「影響されやすい」

　　mental conditioning = brainwashing

29　**proclaim** = declare officially

31　**arrogance** 「傲慢」(adj. arrogant)

Chapter 6 Suicidal Tendencies

EXERCISES

A. Listen and choose the sentence that best describes each picture.

1. (A) (B) (C) (D)   2. (A) (B) (C) (D)

B. Listen to the conversation and choose the best response to each question.

1. What is the man afraid of?

(A) His brother will commit suicide.

(B) His brother suffers from a long illness.

(C) His brother is too nervous.

(D) His brother worries about his future too much.

2. What does the first woman think about the man's brother?

(A) He is weak.

(B) He is spoilt.

(C) He is O.K.

(D) He is pessimistic.

3. What is the second woman's advice?

(A) The man should take his brother to a psychotherapist.

(B) The man should ask someone for help.

(C) The man should leave his brother alone.

(D) The man should be concerned about his brother.

C. Draw lines joining words opposite in meaning.

cause   ·   · impervious
precise   ·   · contempt
admiration   ·   · ancient
modern   ·   · result
susceptible   ·   · inaccurate

Chapter 6 Suicidal Tendencies 41

D. In which order do these sentences form the correct paragraph?

(A) Such actions highlight the urgent need to find peaceful solutions to world problems and to persuade people that such drastic actions are not necessary.

(B) Most people would probably believe that any action designed to make the world a better place would lose its meaning if the person who initiated the action would not live long enough to enjoy the perceived benefits of action.

(C) This is why the news that some people are still willing to take part in an such action is both shocking and hard to comprehend.

(D) To sacrifice one's own life for a cause is something that very few people are willing to do in recent times.

E. Translate the following sentences into English.

(1) 都市部では思春期の青少年の自殺の割合が増加しています.

The suicide rate of _____

_____.

(2) 異なった考え方や価値観を持った異文化について学ぶのはおもしろいです.

_____

_____ and sense

of values.

Chapter 7

Behind the Veil

The success of feminist ideas has, in general, greatly improved the position of women all over the world. Unfortunately, feminism has often clashed with ideas about the role of women in strict Islamic countries like Saudi Arabia, Afghanistan and Iran. In such societies even educated women are not allowed to work or, sometimes, they are not even allowed to drive a car. They are forced to cover their whole bodies with austere clothes, to prevent men seeing any part of their uncovered bodies. They even have to wear veils so that only their eyes are visible. In the home they are under the patriarchal control of their husbands and their husband's word is said to be law.

A strict fundamentalist might, no doubt, defend such behaviour and argue that it was a part of the traditional culture of Islam. However, just because something is a tradition does not make it immune from all criticism. After all, there are good and bad traditions. This is not to say that there exist such things as "absolute good" and "absolute bad."

Rather, we can say that it may be bad for women in that it may prevent them from achieving what they might be capable of achieving and can restrict their independence. Ultimately we could say it is a question of men's control over women, rather than being a specific cultural problem.

Furthermore, the idea that men should be prevented from seeing any part of a woman's unclothed body because men are unable to restrain their uncontrollable and lustful desires is an idea which is deeply insulting to men. One of the things which separates human beings from animals is that human beings have the ability to restrain their most basic urges. It is this self control which makes civilization at all possible.

Nevertheless, this does not mean strict Islamic traditional culture is "bad." It is only bad if a woman who lives in such a society feels she is prevented from doing something (which doesn't harm anyone else) because it is against the beliefs of that culture. If the women of those countries claim to be happy with their situations, we, from other cultures, have no right to criticise those cultures.

NOTES

1 **feminist ideas** = belief in the principle that women should have the same rights and opportunities as men「フェミニズム：男女同権主義」

3 **clash with**「（規則・規律などに）抵触する」

7 **austere** [ɔːstíə]「質素な；飾り気のない」

patriarchal [pèltriάək(ə)l] = ruled or controlled by men

11 **fundamentalist**「（イスラムの）原理主義者」

13 **immune from** ~ = protected or free from ~ (ex. Judging from the circumstances, you won't be immune from prosecution.)

21 **unclothed** = naked「裸の」

22 **restrain**「抑止する」

lustful = filled with a strong sexual desire「好色の」(n. lust)

23 **insulting**「侮辱的な」

25 **urges**「強い衝動」

26 **at all** = in any way；to some extent (ex. Is there any truth at all in what she has just said?)

Chapter 7 Behind the Veil 45

EXERCISES

A. Listen and choose the sentence that best describes each picture.

1. (A) (B) (C) (D)   2. (A) (B) (C) (D)

B. Listen and choose the best response to each question or statement.

1. (A) (B) (C)   2. (A) (B) (C)   3. (A) (B) (C)

C. Draw lines joining words similar in meaning.

defend	·	· control
argue	·	· perfect
restrain	·	· protect
insult	·	· quarrel
absolute	·	· offend

D. In which order do these sentences form the correct paragraph?

(A) Reformists on the other hand tend to be more interested in the process of change and they tend to equate "change" with "improvement" and "tradition" with "stagnation".

(B) However, too rigid an adherence to either a conservative or a reformist viewpoint leads to a simplification of often very complex and confusing problems.

(C) Traditionalists or conservatives tend to value the past and stress that links between the past, present, and future are among the most important aspects of a country's culture.

(D) Perhaps it is wanting "the best of both worlds" to be able to take only the best aspects of these two conflicting viewpoints, but it would be nice if we could.

E. Translate the following Japanese sentences into English.

(1) 世の中には未だに男性の支配下に置かれて，教育を受ける機会を剥奪されている女性たちがいたりします．

Some women _____

are deprived of having an education.

Chapter 7 Behind the Veil

(2)　夫は妻が外で働くことを望むのであれば，それを妨げるべきでは
　　　ありません．

Husband shouldn't prevent _____

_____ .

Chapter 8

Women Are Not from Venus, Men Are Not from Mars

Men and women both come from the planet Earth, of course! A while ago, a number of popular psychology books argued that men and women have a number of fundamental differences and would be best looked at as a completely different species. Men are said to be more interested in competition and power while women are said to be more interested in forming social networks and chatting. While women are said to be more motivated by the need for love and affection, men are said to be more interested in sex. Moreover, the ways that men and women communicate and think, it is claimed, are different.

One interesting aspect about these generalizations made about men and women is that in some ways they are similar to claims made about the characteristics of different nationalities. That is to say, it is not that such generalizations are without any basis in fact, it is just that they too greatly exaggerate certain perceived tendencies. Moreover, such generalizations about men and women confuse behaviour that is socially conditioned and behaviour that is inherent. Furthermore, over- concentration on such perceived "differences" creates a stereotyped image of the typical "man" and "woman," which may be difficult if not impossible for us to live up to.

20   The problem with such stereotypes is that they put limits on what an individual human being can achieve. For example, a young boy might be told "boys shouldn't cry," even though in certain circumstances crying is good for our mental health. A girl might be criticised for being a "tomboy" if she prefers playing games with boys rather than girls. Even adults have certain expectations of "manly" and "womanly" behaviour. In extreme cases we might be forced to suppress important aspects of our own natures in order to comply with social expectations concerning the appropriate behaviour for people of our sex.

    This is not to say that the categories "men" and "women" are meaningless. However, it is sometimes worth wondering why girls are often dressed in pink and boys are often dressed in blue to indicate their sex. After all, there is nothing inherently masculine or feminine about the colours blue and pink.

NOTES

見出し **Women Are Not from Venus, Men Are Not from Mars**（注）John Gray の ベストセラー *MEN ARE FROM MARS, WOMEN ARE FROM VENUS* (1992) をもじったもの.

4   **species**「種」

6   **form social networks**「友達つきあいを広げる」

7   **affection**「愛情」

10   **these generalizations made about ~**「~についてなされた一般化」

12   **That is to say** = which means; namely

12–   **it is not that … it is just that …**「…というわけではなく，…であるにすぎない」(ex. It is not that I don't like the plan, it is just that I can't afford to realize it.)

18–   **if not ~** = although not ~

24   **"tomboy"**「男の子のような女の子；おてんば娘」

26   **suppress**「抑制する；隠す」(ex. The organization tried to suppress the truth about the incident.)

30   **worth ~ ing** = deserving of ~ ing (ex. The scheme is worth trying.)

32   **After all** = in spite of everything「なんといっても」

    inherently = by its or one's nature; intrinsically「本質的に」

Chapter 8 Women Are Not from Venus, Men Are Not from Mars

EXERCISES

A. Listen and choose the sentence that best describes each picture.

1. (A)　(B)　(C)　(D)　　2. (A)　(B)　(C)　(D)

B. Listen to the conversation and choose the best response to each question.

1. What does the woman talk about?

(A)　Her co-worker's husband

(B)　Her co-worker's misunderstanding

(C)　Her co-worker's surprise present

(D)　Her co-worker's joke

52   Cultural Dilemmas

2. What did Mary do?

(A)   She bought a baseball glove for the woman's child.

(B)   She thought the woman's child was a girl

(C)   She associated a boy with baseball.

(D)   She thought girls should not play baseball.

3. What is the stereotyped image based on?

(A)   Gender and food

(B)   Gender and looks

(C)   Gender and activity

(D)   Gender and color

C. Spell out the words defined below.

1.   ( )sy( )ho( )ogy:
      the study of the mind and the way it works and influences
      behavior

2.   c( )m( )e( )ition:
      the struggle between several people or groups to win something

3.   e( )agge( )a( )e:
      to make something seem larger, better, worse, etc., than it really is

4. ( )on( )use:
   to be unable to tell the difference between similar things or people

5. ( )on( )entr( )tion:
   the direction of attention on a single thing, idea, subject, etc.

D. In which order do these sentences form the correct paragraph?

(A) No doubt this is because it seems to be impossible to find non physical characteristics which unite all men and all women equally in separate categories.

(B) The only alternative would be to reject the idea that "men" and "women" can be categorized in any meaningful sense, but this would create futher problems.

(C) To try to overcome this dilemma it is wise to use moderating terms like "have a tendency to" and "tend to" as much as possible.

(D) While most people would probably agree that there are fundamental differences between men and women, it is much more difficult to define what these are.

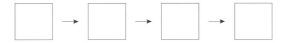

E. Translate the following Japanese sentences into English.

(1) たとえ会社の期待に応えたくても，自らの仕事ぶりを適正に評価されないのならば、その仕事への意欲は減退します.

_____ ,

our motivation will decrease unless our performance is properly assessed.

(2) 男性と女性は本来同じであるにもかかわらず，社会が両者の差異化を図ったりしています.

Men and women are inherently the same, _____

_____ .

Chapter 9

Crime and Punishment

A group of tourists was once surprised to be given the following information by a Singaporean tour guide. He told them that in Singapore elementary school children are taken to see criminals in prison. Once the children see how terrible the conditions in the prison are, the guide said, they will be too frightened to ever commit crimes in the future. The strictness of the prisons in Singapore, he maintained, helps to explain the country's very low crime rate. In this case, we can see how a strict prison system acts not only to punish criminals, but also how it acts as a deterrent to dissuade other people from committing crimes.

How about you? Are you a conservative who supports a strict prison system that punishes criminals? Or, are you a liberal who sees the criminal as a "victim" of social forces whom the prison system should reform or re-educate so that the prisoner can return to society?

The French philosopher Michel Foucault has written interestingly about crime and punishment. He has shown that in the West the way that prisoners are treated has changed over the centuries. At one time prisoners were publicly punished or executed before crowds of people. Many of the people who witnessed these punishments saw them as a form of entertainment. Nowadays, when someone is executed, he or she is put to death by the authorities under conditions of great secrecy. This creates a strange situation in those countries which still maintain the death penalty. Although the death penalty is felt to be necessary, the authorities seem to be too embarrassed to execute people openly these days!

The question of the "rehabilitation" of criminals is also difficult. It has even been argued that the liberal idea of rehabilitation of criminals is actually an infringement of the prisoner's human rights. According to this argument, rehabilitation of a criminal in order to "brainwash" him or her into living in a law-abiding manner interferes with the person's right to decide for him or herself between right and wrong.

Those who have studied prison systems have offered us no convenient solutions to the problem of crime. However, they have proved that crime and its relationship to society is a more complex problem than we might have thought. Our concept of what constitutes "crime" and what constitutes "normal behavior" may have more to do with the culture or period in history we live in than with any more objective truth.

NOTES

- **commit** = perpetrate「(罪・過失などを) 犯す」
- **deterrent**「引き止めるもの：妨害物」
- **dissuade from ...**「…を思いとどまらせる」(ex. He dissuaded his son from quitting school.)
- **reform**「更生させる」
- **Michel Foucault**「ミシェル・フーコー」フランスの哲学者.『監獄の誕生―監視と処罰』は，1975年に出版されている.
- **rehabilitation**「社会復帰」
- **infringement of human rights**「人権侵害」
- **law-abiding**「法律を遵守する：順法精神のある」
- **constitute**「…の構成要素となる；…とみなされる」

Chapter 9 Crime and Punishment

EXERCISES

A. Listen and choose the sentence that best describes each picture.

1. (A)   (B)   (C)   (D)   2. (A)   (B)   (C)   (D)

B. Listen and choose the best response to each question or statement.

1. (A)   (B)   (C)   2. (A)   (B)   (C)   3. (A)   (B)   (C)

C. Draw lines joining words similar in meaning.

terrible · · awful
reform · · jail
entertainment · · penalize
punish · · amusement
prison · · improve

D. In which order do these sentences form the correct paragraph?

(A) In an attempt to prevent crime, modern parks in large cities are now designed to restrict privacy.

(B) In other words, there are no sheltered areas where we can escape the eyes of others.

(C) It has even become difficult for children to find places to play hide-and seek.

(D) But we have to ask ourselves if this is good for us.

E. Translate the following Japanese sentences into English.

(1) 多くの人が，彼がその犯罪を犯すのを目撃しました．

Many people _____ .

（2）　彼女の父親は今服役中であるとの噂を耳にしたのですが，本当で
すか.

Is the _____ ?

Chapter 10

All Jamaicans Love Reggae Music

All Jamaicans love reggae music. All Frenchmen are romantic. All Brazilians can dance the samba. All Chinese can speak Chinese. All Englishmen are gentlemen. All Scotsmen wear kilts, and all Americans like hamburgers. You are probably familiar with such generalizations. There is some truth in such statements. For example, there may be many Englishmen who are gentlemen. However, what about those Englishmen who are soccer hooligans?

Such generalizations can also be found in a certain kind of joke. For example, some customers in a restaurant find flies in their soup. The Americans take the owners to court and win lots of money. The Japanese take memorial photographs standing next to the flies. The Chinese assume they are part of the meal and eat them. Finally, the British say "We won't complain, we just will never come here again." The punch line of this joke makes the point that the British tend to be shy and don't like to make a fuss in public. Although such jokes rely on stereotypes most people would probably not find them too offensive.

What is offensive is when someone refuses to accept that their generalizations are stereotypes, but treat them as true facts about other nationalities. One simple way of stressing that there are always exceptions to the rule in the case of national stereotypes is by playing the "Who says?" game.

To play the "Who says?" game you have to have personal knowledge concerning someone from another or your own country. For example you might know a particularly outgoing girl then you could make the following kind of statement: "Who says all Japanese girls are shy? Have you met my friend Michiko?" Or, "Who says all Americans like Hamburgers? My friend Mike is a vegetarian." This is a very simple and effective way of stressing exceptions to a popular generalization.

You might ask why bother to challenge such statements which after all contain a certain degree of truth. The reason is that the questioning of over-generalizations about anything is, or should be, one of the main purposes of education. Be careful to qualify your generalizations sometimes. Then, to be on the safe side, qualify them again. If you are lucky they might even cease being generalizations after all!

NOTES

見出し **Jamaicans**「ジャマイカ人」（ジャマイカは西インド諸島（West Indies）中の島で連邦邦内の独立国．首都は Kingston）

Reggae [régeɪ] **Music** 「（ジャマイカで生まれた）レゲエ音楽」

7– **soccer hooligans** = supporters who behave violently during or after a soccer game

10 **take ~ to court** = sue ~「に対して訴訟を起こす」

14 **punch line** = the last few words of a joke or story which give it humor

makes the point that = says that ~; explains that ~

15 **makes a fuss** = to be angry or complain

22 **"Who says?" game**「〈~ と言ってるのはだあれ？〉ゲーム固定観念にもとづいたある国民に対するイメージをとりあげ，「と言ってるのはだあれ？」と尋ね，その直後に，そのイメージを打ち砕く例外的な人の事例をあげる，という遊び．

24 **outgoing**「社交性に富んだ」

29 **challenge ~**「真偽を確かめる」

Chapter 10 All Jamaicans Love Reggae Music

31 **over-generalizations**「過度の一般化に対して疑問をもったりすること」
32 **qualify**「適正と判断する」
33 **on the safe side** = taking no risks (ex. Just to be on the safe side, I double-checked these figures on the balance sheet.)
34 **cease** [síːs] = to stop

EXERCISES

A. Listen and choose the sentence that best describes each picture.

1. （A）　（B）　（C）　（D）　2. （A）　（B）　（C）　（D）

64   Cultural Dilemmas

B. Listen to the conversation and choose the best response to each question.

1. Where does this conversation possibly take place?

   (A) In an overseas university
   (B) In a Japanese office
   (C) In a Japanese university
   (D) In an overseas office

2. What surprises the woman?

   (A) Most Japanese people are very punctual
   (B) Some Japanese people are not as punctual as expected
   (C) Some Japanese people come too early
   (D) Many Japanese people are not very strict about punctuality

3. What is important to understand about national stereotypes?

   (A) To know that they do not apply to many people
   (B) To know that they apply to a certain group of people
   (C) To know that they do not apply to some people
   (D) To know that they apply to exceptional people

C. Draw lines joining words opposite in meaning.

raw · · lose
win · · cooked
shy · · accept
refuse · · begin
cease · · outgoing

D. In which order do these sentences form the correct paragraph?

(A) After all, an approximation to the truth could probably be said to be better than no truth at all?

(B) This is because our knowledge of the world can only be partial.

(C) Although we should try to avoid using stereotypes and generalizations as much as possible, it is impossible to avoid using them altogether.

(D) Nevertheless, when we are trying to communicate seriously, we should constantly be seeking to test the validity of the stereotypes we hold about all manner of things.

E. Translate the following Japanese sentences into English.

(1) 一般的にステレオタイプは否定的な意味でとらえられる傾向にありますが，たとえば，いち早く傾向を察知して，インフルエンザの蔓延を予防するのに寄与できるメリットもあります．

People tend to view stereotypes negatively; however, they also

have advantages such as providing people with facts about the flu

so that _____ .

(2) ある人々は彼らが信じていることが常に正しいと思いこんでいて，そのような人々はしばしば他の人も彼らに同意するように要求します．

Some people always assume that what they believe is always right

and _____ .

Chapter 11

The Internet

It is safe to say that the Internet has become massive. During the early stages of computer development, few people could use a computer, since they had to understand a computer language beforehand. But this difficulty was soon overcome, so the Internet grew dramatically in the 1990s. It is said that today (as of 2017) almost 50% of the world's population use the Internet.

As it is the world's main international language, it is probably no surprise that the majority language of the Internet is English, with 27% usage. Nevertheless, quite a lot of Japanese speakers (5%) also use it in their own language. In fact, Asia has the largest number of Internet users, with 42% using a wide variety of languages (including English).

An additional variable to language is gender. Though there is a tendency to think many more men than women use the Internet, in fact, men are only slightly ahead. The biggest gender difference seems to be the type of usage: generally, men use the Internet more for business reasons while women are more interested in the social side of things.

As noted previously, the Internet has grown one hundred times as big as in 1995. Many people think it has been a huge merit to human life, stimulating and freeing our thinking. However, some people believe the Internet is making us more foolish, by interfering with the brain's memory system.

Certainly, there are many good things about the Internet. People can make friends all around the world using social media such as Facebook or Twitter. With these and other online systems, people can find some new ways to socialize with others. It is also common to use the World Wide Web to check the weather or the news, and it is even possible to watch TV by live streaming on the Internet, so we are no longer limited to the regular television or the radio. Though some newspapers don't let you read for free, it is also possible to access mainstream newspapers.

However, there are some negative aspects or dangers to the Internet as well. Spending too much time on the Internet is not good for us, potentially causing an Internet Addiction Disorder. When suffering from this condition, a person may be incapable of communicating with others except through a keyboard. Though you may not need to go to university, as you could do everything over the Internet, it is good for you to meet and interact with other students. Without such contacts, a person may become socially dysfunctional, with problems in communication style, loneliness, inability to recognize appropriate communication content, and so on. Under this situation, people often say more than they should on the Internet.

Then there is the problem of surveillance. Hackers, governments, even major businesses are frequently trying to access information that you may wish to keep private. So, as the famous Orwellian novel 1984 predicted, Big Brother is watching you! Originally it was thought the Internet was free and private, but thanks to whistleblowers such as

Chapter 11 The Internet

Edward Snowden we now know that people are watching us. Though it would take an extremely large number of people to monitor the Internet completely, there are certain keywords which trigger a search into an individual's online behavior. These keywords may "flag" a certain website or hacker into spying on you, even though you don't know it. So though it is a joke, it is no joke: "I'm not paranoid, I just think someone is watching me!"

In addition to such invasions of privacy, some countries censor the Internet directly. For instance, in China, North Korea and Saudi Arabia the government does not allow you to go to certain sites. Some types of information postings are banned, although these are usually things that are banned in society in general. Since these laws may have been created before the arrival of the Internet, it is always a good idea to review relevant local laws before trying to post or access information.

NOTES

- **an additional variable**「もう一つの追加要素」
- **Internet Addiction Disorder**「インターネット依存症」
- **dysfunctional**「機能不全の；機能を果していない」
- **surveillance**「監視」
- **Big Brother is watching you!**
  Big Brother とは，ジョージ・オーウェル作の SF 小説『1984』に登場する支配者のこと。"Big Brother is watching you." とは，「政府や権力者が全ての人々を監視している」という意味。
- **whistleblower**「不正を告発する人；告発者」
- **Edward Snowden**「エドワード・スノーデン」

エドワード・スノーデンは，アメリカの国家安全保障局（NSA）の局員という立場を利用して，PRISMという NSA の国家規模の監視プログラムの存在を暴露した．具体的にはインターネットや携帯電話のネットワークでやりとりされる膨大な情報を様々な方法で傍受・解析し，ありとあらゆるターゲットについての個人情報を収集していたとされている．

- **trigger**「引き起こす；もたらす；きっかけとなる」
- **spy on**「密かに見張る；探る」
- **paranoid**「疑い深い；誇大妄想的な；考えすぎ」
- **ban** = forbid

EXERCISES

A. Listen and choose the sentence that best describes each picture.

1. (A)　(B)　(C)　(D)　　2. (A)　(B)　(C)　(D)

B. Listen and choose the best response to each question or statement.

1. (A)　(B)　(C)　　2. (A)　(B)　(C)　　3. (A)　(B)　(C)

C. Spell out the words defined below.

1. ( )oo( )is( ):
   to have or show a lack of good sense or judgement

2. ( )o( )u( )at( )on:
   the number of people living in a particular area

3. a( )a( )e:
   to have knowledge, perception or realization of a situation

Chapter 11 The Internet 71

4. i( )ca( )a( )l( ):
   unable to do or achieve something

5. b( )( ):
   to say that something must not be done, seen or used

D. In which order do these sentences form a correct paragraph?

(A) Using this convenience, students obtain credits to graduate by taking these classes and submitting papers.

(B) Have you heard of N High School, an online high school founded by the media company, Kadokawa Dwango Corporation, in 2016?

(C) It provides more than two thousand students with online video classes which they can watch on a PC or smartphone at home, or wherever they like.

(D) In addition, students can also experience homeroom and club activities on the Internet!

E. Translate the following Japanese sentences into English.

(1) 情報が検閲されている国があることは広く知られていますが，世界中でわれわれが入手できる情報はある程度操作されていることも知っておくべきです．

Although it is widely known that there are some countries where the information is censored, we should also be aware of the fact that _____ .

(2) インターネットを活用すれば多大な利便性に与れる一方で，絶えずネット媒介の詐欺に遭遇する危険性も否定できません．

_____ ,

we cannot rule out the danger of being under the threat of fraud through internet shopping.

Chapter 12

Living on Fiji Time

A man from Fiji once said that in his country it is necessary to provide delicious food in order to get anyone to attend business meetings. He also said that Fijians tend to have a loose sense of time. For example, if a meeting is scheduled for 8 a.m., people might not arrive until about 8:30 a.m. or later. Such a relaxed attitude to time might bother someone from, for example, Germany, where people tend to be very strict about punctuality. On the other hand, people who live in cultures where the pace of life is more relaxed, like Fiji, might find the effort to keep strictly to a rigid timetable equally stressful.

There is a well-known story concerning the Beatles visit to Japan in the 1960s. It is said that the schedule drawn up for the Beatles was very strict. The times for everything, even the number of seconds the Beatles would spend in the lift were listed. One of the Beatles, according to the story, deliberately pressed the "stop" button in the lift, perhaps in protest at the overly strict schedule!

These days, our lives are increasingly ruled by the clock. Many people lack the time to have a "proper" breakfast as they rush to work. In Britain a proper breakfast used to include fried eggs, bacon, tomatoes, sausage and mushrooms, as well as toast and milk tea. Nowadays, few
20 people have the time to prepare and enjoy such a breakfast, and most people usually have a light meal of toast or cereal and tea as they rush to work in the mornings.

Only on holiday can we enjoy a more relaxed pace, but it might be necessary to go to a remote area to do so. Once on holiday on a
25 small island in the Orkneys off the coast of Scotland, I went to do a little shopping in the few shops in the village. To buy the few goods I wanted, something which would take me less than five minutes in a modern supermarket, took me most of the morning. The reason was that it was the custom in the village to have a long chat with the
30 shopkeepers of every shop one visited. To do your shopping quickly would have been considered very rude. Shopping was considered more than simply a purchase of materials. It was considered an important social activity and an important means of transmitting information in an isolated community. And, as long as you were not in a hurry, it was fun!

NOTES

3 **Fijians**「フィジー諸島の人々」
loose [lúːs] = not exact; vague
7 **punctuality** = being on time
rigid = stiff「硬直な；厳密な；頑なな」
13 **lift** = elevator（米）（cf. tube（英）= subway（米））
14 **deliberately** = on purpose; intentionally
15 **in protest at ~** =protesting at ~

overly =too; very much
24 **remote**「遠くはなれた；へんぴな」
25 **Orkneys** =Orkney Islands「オークニー諸島」スコットランド北方の群島.
25 **off the coast**「沖合いに」
transmitting「伝える；行き渡らせる」(n. transmission)

Chapter 12 Living on Fiji Time

EXERCISES

A. Listen and choose the sentence that best describes each picture.

1. (A) (B) (C) (D)   2. (A) (B) (C) (D)

B. Listen to the questions and circle the correct answer.

Q1: _____
_____

(A) No one would show up at 8 o'clock.
(B) Everyone would come on time.
(C) They would prepare a delicious breakfast for the meeting.

Q2: _____

(A) Because he wanted to get out of the lift.
(B) Because he wanted to find out how long it took to stop the lift.
(C) Because he wanted to protest the strict schedule.

Q3: _____

(A)   Less than five minutes.

(B)   Most of the morning.

(C)   All day long.

C. Draw lines joining words opposite in meaning.

relaxed ·	· polite
punctual ·	· customer
light ·	· tense
shopkeeper ·	· late
rude ·	· heavy

D. In which order do these sentences form the correct paragraph?

(A) One of the paradoxes about time is that while most people don't enjoy the sensation of being bored, neither would they like their lives to flash by in an instant of total pleasure.

(B) Strangely enough it does seem possible to "slow down time" by concentrating very intensely on what one is doing to the point that you "create" a new sense of time.

(C) In a sense this is what happens when people successfully meditate and such people often speak of having "made time stand still."

(D) Have you ever felt that time is a very mysterious thing that seems to speed up or down according to what you are doing and how you are feeling?

E.　Translate the following Japanese sentences into English.

（1）イスラム教徒の人たちが時間にルーズであると評する人たちは，「明日のわが身は神のみぞしる」というインシャラーの理念（Inshallah's teachings）を理解していないからです．

_____

fail to understand Inshallah's teachings that 'Only God knows what happens next'.

（2）スローライフという概念は，ゆっくりと食事をしたり，ショッピングを楽しんだりするなど，時間をかけて人生を楽しみ，生活の質を重視することを意味します．

The concept of the 'Slow life' means taking time and enjoying our life, such as by eating as well as shopping, in which _____

_____ .

Chapter 13

Affirmative Action

Not so long ago, Texas Law School established and executed lower score standards for African-American and Mexican-American applicants. In addition, the school set up a separate review of those applicants, in order to achieve a 10 percent Mexican-American enrollment and a 5 percent enrollment of black students. Four non-minority group applicants challenged the policy, claiming the quota system violated their rights. A trial court agreed, and on subsequent appeal, the appeals court went further ruling 'the law school may not use race as a factor in law school admissions.' When Susan heard this ruling, she nodded in approval, glancing at her three children who were playing nearby.

Each of the three children has a different father. The eldest daughter, Barbara, has a third-generation Japanese-American father. (Susan divorced him). The second daughter, Julie, had a white American father who died of an illness shortly after Julie's birth. Susan then married a Mexican and her first son, Albert, was born last year. Susan herself is a white American. 'It is just not right that family members should be classified by race,' she said with anger.

The first time the phrase 'Affirmative Action' was used was in a Presidential Executive Order of March 1961, when President J. F. Kennedy ordered that federal contractors take affirmative action to ensure that 'the contractor will, in all solicitations or advertisements for employees placed by or on the behalf of the contractor, state that all qualified applicants will receive considerations for employment without regard to race, creed, color, or national origin'(Executive Order 10925).

Originally, Kennedy hoped that 'affirmative steps' would be taken to protect individuals from hidden forms of discrimination against African Americans and, in many cases, Asians. Discrimination has been concealed behind the phrase 'Affirmative Action.'

With the above situation as a background, a call for 'correction for excessive equality' has been heard in the last few years in the US. The Dean of the University of California (UC) said on TV, 'Preferring one group of applicants has led to discrimination against other groups. The UC board of directors has decided to abolish all forms of favorable treatment according to race, creed, and sex.''Right on' said Susan, to the surprise of her children.

In the future, those from widely different racial and ethnic backgrounds will be mixing with others. In Japan the number of people from different countries will increase. What about 'Affirmative Action' in Japan?

NOTES

- **Affirmative Action**
  「(米) 非白人少数民族や女性の雇用促進計画：少数派優遇策」
  弱者集団の不利な現状を，歴史的経緯や社会環境に鑑みた上で是正するための改善措置のこと．この場合の是正措置とは，民族や人種や出自による差別と貧困に悩む被差別集団の進学や就職や職場における昇進においての特別な採用枠の設置や試験点数の割り増しなどの直接の優遇措置を指す．
- **execute** 「実施する」
- **quota system** 「割当制度」

Chapter 13 Affirmative Action

- **trial court** 「第一審裁判所」
- **subsequent** = following 「次の」
- **appeals court** 「(米) 高等裁判所，控訴 [上訴] 裁判所」
  予審裁判所からの上訴 (appeals) を審理する裁判所．
- **ruling** 「判定；裁定」
- **solicitation** 「懇請 (すること)」
- **Executive Order** 「(米) 大統領令，または州知事命令」
  大統領または州知事が議会の承認を要せずに発する命令で法律と同じ効果を持つ．
- 10 **board of directors** 「取締役会」

EXERCISES

A. Listen and choose the sentence that best describes each picture.

1.　(A)　(B)　(C)　(D)　　2.　(A)　(B)　(C)　(D)

B. Listen and choose the best response to each question or statement.

1.　(A)　(B)　(C)　　2.　(A)　(B)　(C)　　3.　(A)　(B)　(C)

C. Spell out the words defined below.

1. en( )ol( )m( )nt:
   the number of people who have arranged to join a school or a class

2. ( )a( )e:
   a group of people sharing the same culture, history or language

3. cla( )( )if( ):
   to consider (someone or something) as belonging to a particular group

4. ( )is( )rim( )nat( )on:
   the practice of treating a person or a group differently from another in an unfair way

5. a( )o( )is( ):
   to officially end a law or a system

D. In which order do these sentences form the correct paragraph?

(A) In the 1970s, the Malaysian government implemented affirmative action policies for 'bumiputras,' in other words Malays and other indigenous peoples of Malaysia.

(B) Therefore, she decided to study at a university in the UK; she later became a lawyer to help refugees.

(C) These policies have sometimes prevented non-Malays from receiving public education and national scholarships.

Chapter 13 Affirmative Action 83

（D）For instance, one of my friends, Shook Yee, wasn't accepted by a Malaysian national university—even though she was an excellent student—because she is Chinese-Malaysian, not a bumiputra.

☐ → ☐ → ☐ → ☐

E. Translate the following Japanese sentences into English.

（1） 経営陣を代表して，CEO（最高経営責任者）は，これまで女性より男性を多く採用してきた会社方針を改めることを表明しました．

On behalf of the management, _____

_____ which currently led to more men

than women being hired.

（2） 米国では，積極的差別解消策の導入によって逆差別の問題が表面化したため，それを撤廃する州が相次いでいます．

In the United States, because _____ ,

_____ ,

more and more states are eliminating it.

Chapter 14

The Diversity of Lying

Most parents scold their children when they tell lies, but all children grow up to become liars anyway! This is because being able to tell a good lie in certain circumstances is an important social skill. For example, if your friend asks you what you think of his/her new hairstyle, even if you hate it, would you say so? Most people in this situation would probably tell a lie so as not to hurt their friend's feelings. It is certainly true that a person who is too honest is likely to have few friends. On the other hand, nobody likes a person who tells too many lies either. Perhaps your future success in life will mainly depend on how skillfully you learn the system of lying.

Of course, not all lies are the same. In English a "white lie" is a lie made in the better interests of something or someone other than the liar. Although a white lie is still technically a lie, it is not considered to be as bad as some other kinds of lies. The lies people in love often tell each other are also easily forgiven, because the condition of being in love is seen as a kind of illness which blinds people to everyday realities.

The lies that politicians make during election campaigns are another category of "semi" lies. For example, a certain politician might find that what he promised is either impossible or not sensible. By turning his pre-election promise into a lie through not carrying it out, we could say that the politician was simply making the compromises and practicing the pragmatism which is politics. More cynically, we could say that the politician was a dishonest liar who would promise you anything to get your vote!

This is the problem with lying. Because in some situations it is impossible to tell with absolute certainty whether someone is lying or telling the truth, we ourselves are forced to become the ultimate judge of what is the truth and what is a lie. You could say that in this situation we create truth and untruth. On the other hand, perhaps this is just another lie!

NOTES

- **diversity**「多様性（許容）；さまざまな種類」
- **white lie**「罪のない嘘」
- **make a compromise** 「妥協する」
- **pragmatism**「現実主義；実用（実利）主義」
- **cynically** 「皮肉なことに」
- **dishonest** 「不正直な；誠意を感じられない；いい加減な」(n. dishonesty)
- **certainty** = a sure fact
- **ultimate** = final ; coming at the end

Chapter 14 The Diversity of Lying   87

EXERCISES

A. Listen and choose the sentence that best describes each picture.

1. (A) (B) (C) (D)   2. (A) (B) (C) (D)

B. Listen and choose the best response to each question or statement.

1. (A) (B) (C)   2. (A) (B) (C)   3. (A) (B) (C)

C. Spell out the words defined below.

1. dsocl:

   to speak in an angry or a critical way to someone who has done something wrong

2. utrh:

   to cause pain or injury to yourself, someone else, or to a part of your body

3. inlcoaipit:
someone who works in politics, especially an elected member of the government

4. ehsitndso:
saying or likely to say things that are untrue

5. tlsboeau:
something that is always true and does not change

D. In which order do these sentences form the correct paragraph?

(A) According to psychologists, telling their first believable lie signals an important stage in the child's mental development.

(B) Actually, you probably can't. Research shows that even parents, and social workers who work with children every day, often cannot tell when kids are lying.

(C) Don't worry too much about it, though.

(D) Do you think you can detect a child's lies?

Chapter 14 The Diversity of Lying

E. Translate the following Japanese sentences into English.

（1）　嘘つきは，たとえ本当のことをいったとしても信じてもらえない
　　　ことがあります.

　　　It is likely that nobody would _____

　　　_____ .

（2）　諺にもあるように，『嘘も方便』なのです.

　　　_____ .

Chapter 15

Talking With a Child About Cancer

"I feel great when I am listening to the sound of the waves here!" said the young boy at Malibu Beach. "I also like Salt Lake City, but I am very glad to be here. I really like this place. The beach is so beautiful, and the sea seems to stretch out till it meets the sky. It's really mysterious."

The boy's name is Jack. He is eight years old and he is very ill. At the age of six his illness was diagnosed as hepatoma, or childhood liver cancer. Hepatoma is a rare disease in which cancer cells are found in the tissues of a child's liver. Two types of cancer start in the liver, hepatoblastoma and hepatocellular cancer. These are differentiated by the appearance of the cancer cells under a microscope. Hepatoblastoma is more common in young children before the age of three and may be caused by an abnormal gene. Children infected with hepatitis B or C (viral infections of the liver) are more likely than other children to get hepatocellular cancer. Hepatocellular cancer is generally found in children from birth to age four, but can also be found in older children.

Two years have gone by since Jack's doctor said, "He has less than one year to live." The doctor told the boy and his parents about the illness when he discovered that it was terminal. Jack has understood the precise nature of his illness from the beginning. He is willing to accept treatment and tries hard to live longer. One day he said to his parents, "I want to go to Malibu Beach and stay there for some time." He intuitively felt that he might die soon. His parents decided to sell their house in Salt Lake City and buy a house at Malibu Beach. They asked a real estate company in the Malibu Beach area to find them a house. The widow of a rich man who heard about their reason for moving said that she was willing to offer her cottage to the family for free. Jack's parents gratefully accepted this kind offer and moved to Malibu Beach from Salt Lake City.

A doctor tells a six-year-old child that the child is suffering from childhood cancer. This child, when he is told about his disease, begins to realize that he will soon die but does not give up hope to the end. His mother continues to give loving and delicate terminal care to her child every day.

When one compares the reality in America with the situation in Japan, one cannot help but wonder if the current Japanese system for treating a childhood cancer is really suitable. A child with cancer often believes that his illness is a punishment for something he has done wrong. The child may feel unnecessary anxiety and guilt. Health professionals generally agree that telling a child the truth about his disease decreases his anxiety and prevents him from feeling guilty. Also, knowing the truth increases the child's cooperation with his treatment. Can doctors in Japan tell a six-year-old child that he is suffering from childhood cancer? Can the child's parents endure such news? Just how well is the need for terminal care for children understood in Japan?

On the beach at Malibu, Jack's mother says, "If possible, I want my child to spend his last moments with his head in my lap." Her

Chapter 15 Talking With a Child About Cancer   93

eight-year-old son listens and slowly nods his head while he sits facing a fresh wind from the sea.

NOTES

- **Malibu Beach**「マリブビーチ」
  太平洋を一望できる絶景ビーチ．サンタモニカの近くにありながらも，観光地化されておらず，ゆったりと過ごすことができる．
- **was diagnosed as...**「…であると診断された」
- **hepatoma**「肝細胞癌」
- **cell**「細胞」
- **tissue**「組織」
- **hepatoblastoma**「肝細胞芽腫」
- **hepatocellular**「肝細胞の」
- **gene**「遺伝子」
- **hepatitis B or C**「B型肝炎あるいはC型肝炎」
- **viral infection**「ウィルス感染」
- **intuitively**「本能的に；直観的に」
- **widow**「未亡人」⇔ widower
- **treatment**「治療法」
- **endure** = bear ; stand

EXERCISES

A. Listen and choose the sentence that best describes each picture.

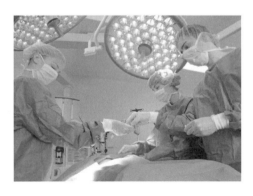

1. (A)　(B)　(C)　(D)　　2. (A)　(B)　(C)　(D)

B. Listen and choose the best response to each question or statement.

1. (A) (B) (C)   2. (A) (B) (C)   3. (A) (B) (C)

C. Draw lines joining words similar in meaning.

rare　　　　·　　　·　worry
precise　　·　　　·　unusual
grateful　　·　　　·　accurate
anxiety　　·　　　·　extend
stretch　　·　　　·　appreciative

D. In which order do these sentences form the correct paragraph?

(A) For these reasons, some medical institutions have started to offer home care for children with terminal cancer, so that they can spend more time with their families.

(B) Children with cancer are often treated in hospitals that are far away from their families.

(C) Naturally this usually makes it difficult for their parents to visit them.

(D) Moreover, since children are not allowed into hospital wards, they can't see their siblings during their hospitalization.

Chapter 15 Talking With a Child About Cancer   95

E. Translate the following Japanese sentences into English.

（1）　インフォームドコンセントの考え方は，日本社会でも次第に浸透
してきています.

The perceptions of informed consent _____

_____ .

（2）　体に傷があると，ウィルスや細菌に感染しやすくなります.

_____if we

have a cut on our body.

執筆者一覧

淺 間 正 通
荒 尾 浩 子
伊 東 田 恵
大 橋 由紀子
古 西 美佐子
小 林 猛 久
西 村 厚 子
安 冨 勇 希
Colin Sloss

執筆協力者

猪口　綾奈
Blair Thomson
Nicholas Lumbert

Cultural Dilemmas
　Controversial Issues To Stretch Your Mind
『異文化の戸惑い』

| 2018 年 3 月 30 日　初　版 | 2019 年 1 月 15 日　第 2 刷 |

| 編著者 | 淺　間　正　通 |
| | C o l i n　S l o s s |

発行者　佐 々 木　　元

発行所 株式会社 英　宝　社

　(〒 101-0032)　東京都千代田区岩本町 2-7-7
　☎ [03] (5833) 5870-1　Fax [03] (5833) 5872

ISBN 978-4-269-14038-7 C1082　[印刷・製本／モリモト印刷株式会社]